STUPENDOUS AND TREMENDOUS TECHNOLOGY

MEGA (AND MIGHTY) MACHINES

ENTER A WORLD OF MOMENTOUS MECHANICALS!

CLAUDIA MARTIN

Please visit our website, www.garethstevens.com. For a free color catalog of all our high-quality books, call toll free 1-800-542-2595 or fax 1-877-542-2596.

Published in 2025 by
Gareth Stevens Publishing
2544 Clinton St.
Buffalo, NY 14224

First published in Great Britain in 2022 by Wayland

Author and editor:
Claudia Martin

Series designer:
Rocket Design (East Anglia) Ltd

Illustrator:
Steve Evans

Proofreader:
Annabel Savery

Cataloging-in-Publication Data

Names: Martin, Claudia.
Title: Mega (and mighty) machines / Claudia Martin.
Description: Buffalo, NY : Gareth Stevens Publishing, 2025. | Series: Stupendous and tremendous technology | Includes glossary and index.
Identifiers: ISBN 9781538294567 (pbk.) | ISBN 9781538294574 (library bound) | ISBN 9781538294581 (ebook)
Subjects: LCSH: Machinery--Juvenile literature.
Classification: LCC TJ147. M37 2025 | DDC 621.8--dc23

Illustrations by Steve Evans: front cover main, 1, 3b, 4cr, 7bl, 9c, 11c, 12cr, 13cr, 14cr, 16cr, 18b, 21tl, 22cr, 23c, 24c, 25tr, 29tl, 29cr, 30br, 31cr, 31br.

Picture acknowledgements: iStock: alexeys 15cr; Shutterstock: VizRad front cover tr, rumruay 2tr, 26bl, VectorMine 3tr, 9tl, 20c, Halfpoint 4bl, CRS Photo 4bc, IMG Stock Studio 4br, Belish 5cl, BigMouse 5cr, mirounga 5bl, LIAL 5bc, Sukpaiboonwat 5br, Sergey Merkulov 6c, 19tl, 26c, Emre Terim 7tr, tele52 7br, BlueRingMedia 8cr, FotoDuets 8bl, Bermek 8br, ChiccoDodiFC 9bl, Anadolu_Dizgi 10c, MOLPIX 10bl, AC Manley 11br, Sata Production 12bc, Alex Mit 12br, Creative Family 13cl, voy ager 13bl, nexus7 13btr, VILevi 13br, Drp8 14bl, 14br, Einar Muoni 15cl, Izabela Magier 15c, Boonyarak voranimmanont 15bl, Rvector 16bl, tersetki 17, dedMazay 19tr, Designua 19bl, Igillustrator 19br, innakreativ 21c, 32cr, sspopov 21cl, musiktej 21bl, BNP Design Studio 22bl, 32br, Sketh Master 23r, Multigon 23bl, 30tl, Chatham172 24bl, John_T 24br, KOKTARO 25bl, Roman Samborskyi 25br, M. Moira 27tr, Macrovector 27b.

All additional design elements from Shutterstock or drawn by designer.

Printed in the United States of America

CPSIA compliance information: Batch #CSGS25: For further information contact Gareth Stevens at 1-800-542-2595.

MEGA MACHINES CONTENTS

MAGNIFICENT MACHINES

From cars to kettles, cranes to drills, machines do useful work in homes, factories, and schools, and on construction sites. People have been using machines for thousands of years, at first to help with simple tasks ...

WHAT IS A MACHINE?

A machine is a human-made device that uses forces – such as a push or a pull – to carry out a physical task, such as lifting a load. Machines are useful because they make work easier. The most basic machines are called simple machines. They are wedges, inclined planes, wheels, levers, pulleys, and screws. Simple machines can change the strength or direction of a force, turning a small movement into a bigger movement or changing a round-and-round motion into an up-and-down motion. More complex machines, called compound machines, often contain several simple machines. Some clever compound machines do the important work of changing one form of energy, such as electricity, into another form of energy, such as movement.

AN AXE IS A SIMPLE MACHINE CALLED A WEDGE THAT MAKES IT EASIER TO DO THE WORK OF CHOPPING DOWN A TREE.

WHAT POWERS MACHINES?

A machine needs energy, or power, so it can move and carry out its work. Today, many machines get their energy from electric motors, but there are lots of other sources of machine power.

PURPOSEFUL PERSON

HUMAN EFFORT PUSHES A WHEELBARROW, WHICH IS AN EXAMPLE OF A SIMPLE MACHINE CALLED A LEVER.

AMAZING ANIMAL

OXEN ARE PULLING ALONG A PLOW, AN EXAMPLE OF A WEDGE, TO TURN OVER THE SOIL.

WONDERFUL WATER

PULLED BY THE FORCE OF GRAVITY, FALLING WATER TURNS A WATERWHEEL, WHICH MOVES MACHINERY TO DO WORK SUCH AS GRINDING FLOUR.

WHAT IS THE WORLD'S BIGGEST MACHINE?

The world's biggest machine is the Large Hadron Collider, which occupies a circular tunnel 17 miles (27 km) across, beneath the France–Switzerland border. It sends tiny particles smaller than atoms, called protons, crashing into each other to see what happens. In contrast, the smallest machines are molecular machines, made of just a few atoms joined together. In the future, molecular machines could carry medicines around the human body to where they are needed.

A Chinese crane called Taisun holds the record for lifting the heaviest load. In 2008, this machine lifted a boat weighing 44,385,667 pounds (20,133,000 kg).

LARGE HADRON COLLIDER

I MAY BE SMALL, BUT I STILL HAVE VERY IMPORTANT WORK TO DO!

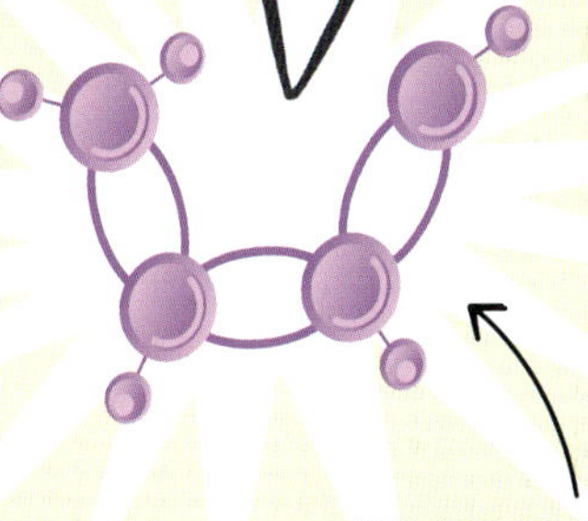

MOLECULAR MACHINE

WILD WIND

WIND SPINS TURBINES, WHICH ARE PARTS OF MACHINES THAT CHANGE MOVEMENT ENERGY INTO ELECTRICITY.

ENERGETIC ENGINE

A CAR GETS THE ENERGY TO TURN ITS WHEELS FROM AN ENGINE THAT BURNS LIQUID FUEL.

MARVELOUS MOTOR

AN ELECTRIC MOTOR TURNS ELECTRICAL ENERGY INTO MOVEMENT.

GETTING MOVING

A machine can't move without energy! Engines and motors are machines that change other forms of energy into movement energy. For example, engines use heat energy to move cars and machinery. Electric motors use electrical energy to power tools and appliances.

HOW DOES AN ENGINE WORK?

An engine usually burns a fuel, such as coal or gasoline, to release heat. However, some engines use the heat of the sun, which creates less pollution than burning fuel. The heat warms a gas, which expands as it gets hotter. One type of engine, called a Stirling engine, uses gas that is sealed inside a chamber in which two pistons can move up and down.

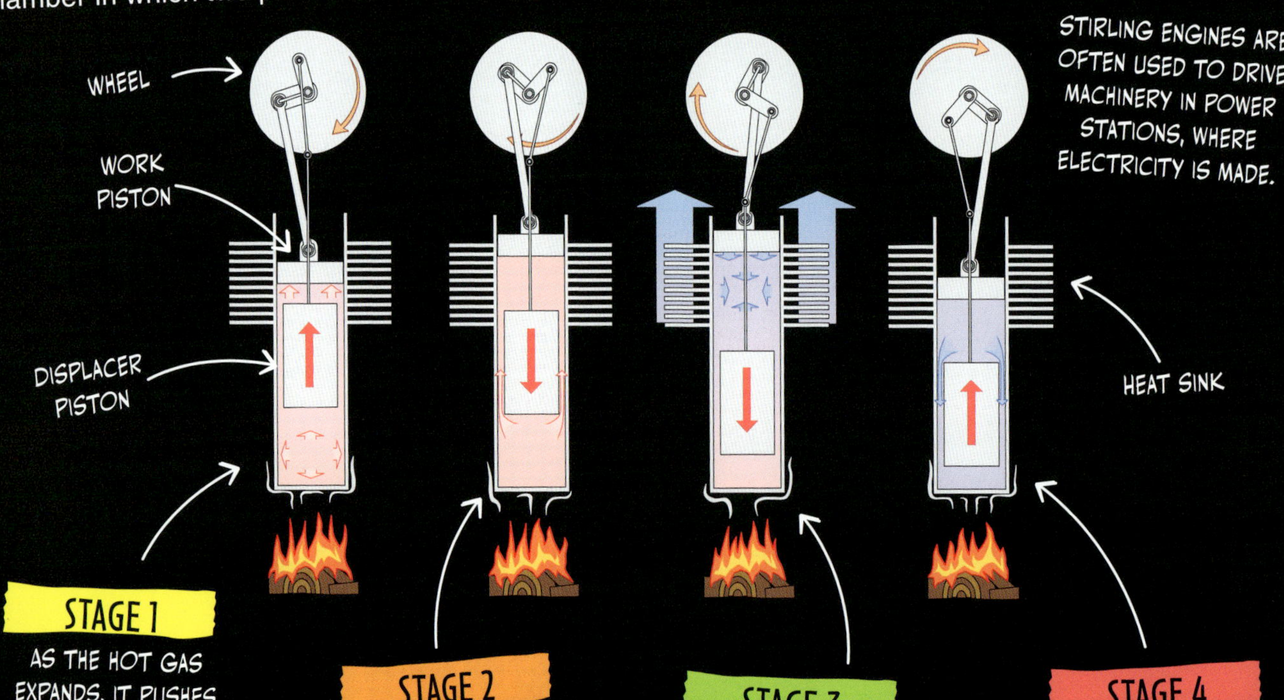

STIRLING ENGINES ARE OFTEN USED TO DRIVE MACHINERY IN POWER STATIONS, WHERE ELECTRICITY IS MADE.

STAGE 1
AS THE HOT GAS EXPANDS, IT PUSHES BOTH THE WORK PISTON AND THE DISPLACER PISTON UPWARD. THE WORK PISTON TURNS A WHEEL THAT DRIVES MACHINERY.

STAGE 2
THE TURNING OF THE WHEEL PUSHES DOWN THE DISPLACER PISTON. HOT GAS MOVES AROUND THE DISPLACER PISTON TO THE TOP END OF THE CHAMBER.

STAGE 3
THE GAS IS COOLED BY A HEAT SINK, USUALLY A METAL GRILL, THAT RELEASES HEAT FROM THE ENGINE.

STAGE 4
AS THE WHEEL TURNS, IT PUSHES THE WORK PISTON DOWNWARD, PUSHING THE GAS BACK TO THE BOTTOM OF THE CHAMBER, WHERE IT IS REHEATED.

WHAT DOES AN ELECTRIC MOTOR DO?

Many of the electrical appliances in your home, from the washing machine to the microwave, are powered by electric motors. But how do they work? Electric motors rely on magnetism. The similar poles of two magnets repel each other, while the opposite poles attract. When electricity runs through a wire, it creates a magnetic field around the wire. If the wire is placed near a magnet, the two will attract or repel each other. This force can be used to create a turning motion, which drives the moving parts of a machine.

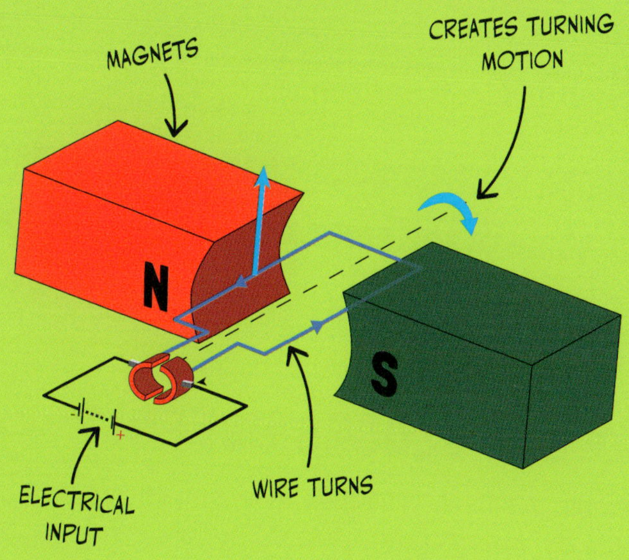

WHICH MACHINES ARE POWERED BY AIR?

Pneumatic motors are powered by air that is compressed (or squeezed), then released so that it creates movement – like a rush of wind. These motors are often used in handheld tools, such as drills, and are safer to use in places where sparks from electrical machines could start a fire. However, the air must first be compressed by a machine that is powered by an electric motor or engine.

Molecular motors are molecules that move when they react to something, such as chemicals or light. Natural molecular motors power everything in our bodies, from muscle movements to transporting materials. Scientists are working on human-made molecular motors, less than a thousandth of the width of a human hair. In the future, molecular motors that react to sunlight could power special fabrics that contract or expand in bright sunlight. They could power sun shades that open on their own!

THE SUN'S GONE IN! REACT, REACT, REACT!

WONDERFUL WEDGES

A wedge is a triangular-shaped simple machine. Around 1.6 million years ago, some of the earliest machines were wedges. Stone axes have a sharp, narrow end and a blunt, thicker end – creating a wonderful wedge!

WHY ARE WEDGES USEFUL?

All simple machines give their user a mechanical advantage. Energy is the ability to do work. It can exist in different forms, such as food or movement. A force transmits energy from one object to another. A simple machine doesn't create energy (nothing can), it just transfers it in a way that is useful. A wedge's shape means the force applied to the wedge (the input force) is less than the resulting force (the output force) – so it takes less energy to do work. This is because the input force (a hammer hitting the wedge) is applied across the broad, flat surface. The energy is transported to the sharp end, where it is concentrated in a smaller area, resulting in a larger but more focused force on the wood being chopped.

WHAT DO WE USE WEDGES FOR?

CUTTING

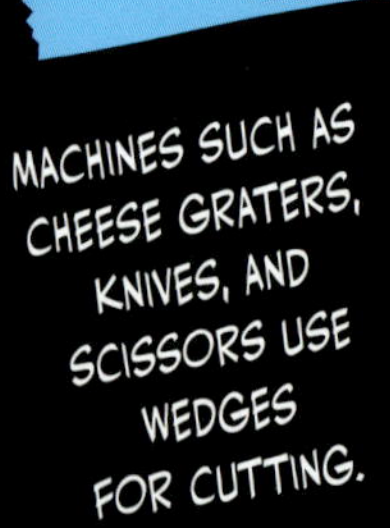

MACHINES SUCH AS CHEESE GRATERS, KNIVES, AND SCISSORS USE WEDGES FOR CUTTING.

HOLDING TOGETHER

ONCE A WEDGE LIKE A PUSHPIN, NAIL, OR DOORSTOP HAS BEEN PUSHED INTO PLACE, IT HOLDS THINGS TOGETHER.

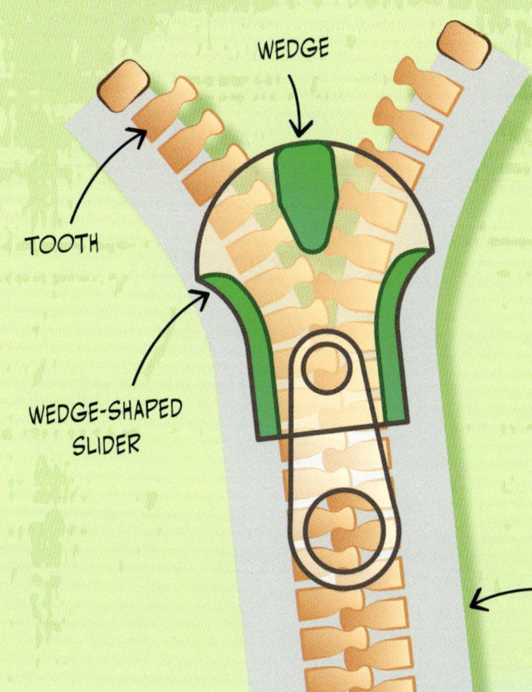

HOW DOES A ZIPPER WORK?

The track of a zipper has two strips of teeth. Each tooth is made up of a hook and a hollow. To close a zipper, each hook has to latch into a hollow in the opposite side of the track. A zipper's slider contains a series of wedges. As a slider closes a zipper, its wedge-shaped edges push sideways on the teeth, latching them together. When a zipper is opened, a plow-shaped wedge is pulled down the tracks, exerting a sideways force and separating the teeth.

BACK IN THE EARLY 20TH CENTURY, THE ZIPPER WAS THE HUGELY SUCCESSFUL INVENTION OF SWEDISH-AMERICAN ENGINEER GIDEON SUNDBACK.

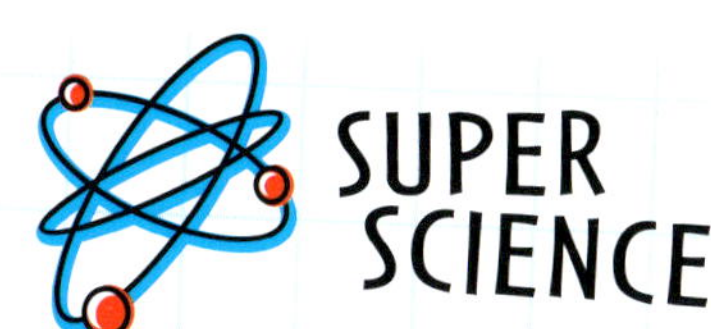

Wedges play an important role in the design of super-fast vehicles. A wedge is an aerodynamic shape, which means it cuts easily through air, just as it cuts easily through wood. Cars, trains, and planes often have wedge-shaped noses. This lowers the resistance of the air to the vehicle's movement, allowing it to travel more quickly.

SCRAPING

THE NARROW EDGE OF THE WEDGE EXERTS AN UPWARD FORCE ON THE SNOW!

THE BLADES OF A SNOWPLOW OR A SHOVEL ARE WEDGES, USED TO SLIDE UNDER AND LIFT A LOAD.

UP THE RAMP!

A ramp – also known as an inclined plane – is a sloping surface. Wheelchair users know how useful inclined planes are, because they make it easier to travel from one level to another. These machines are simple ... but stupendous!

WHAT'S THE ADVANTAGE OF AN INCLINED PLANE?

Like all simple machines, an inclined plane gives its user a mechanical advantage. It takes less force to slide a heavy load up a slope than it does to lift the load to the same height. This is because the inclined plane supports part of the weight of the object as it is pushed up the slope. The shallower (flatter) the angle of the slope, the less force is needed to slide the object up the slope. However, the user needs to move their load over a greater distance – all the way up the long slope, rather than directly upward.

WHAT IS THE STEEPEST RAILWAY?

The steepest railway in the world is the Katoomba Scenic Railway in Australia, which has an angle of 52 degrees. It was originally constructed to lift coal from a mine on the valley floor to the top of a hill. Railways this steep cannot use ordinary tracks and trains, as – thanks to gravity – the trains would need immensely powerful engines to stop them from sliding backward (as well as very good brakes). Katoomba is an incline railway that uses super-strong cables to slide trains up the track.

HOW DOES AN ESCALATOR WORK?

Although an escalator looks very much like moving stairs, it actually works on the same principle as an inclined plane! An escalator is powered by an electric motor (see page 7), which can be less powerful than the motor needed to lift an equal amount of weight directly upward. The motor rotates two sets of tracks – which are moving inclined planes. The tracks move the steps.

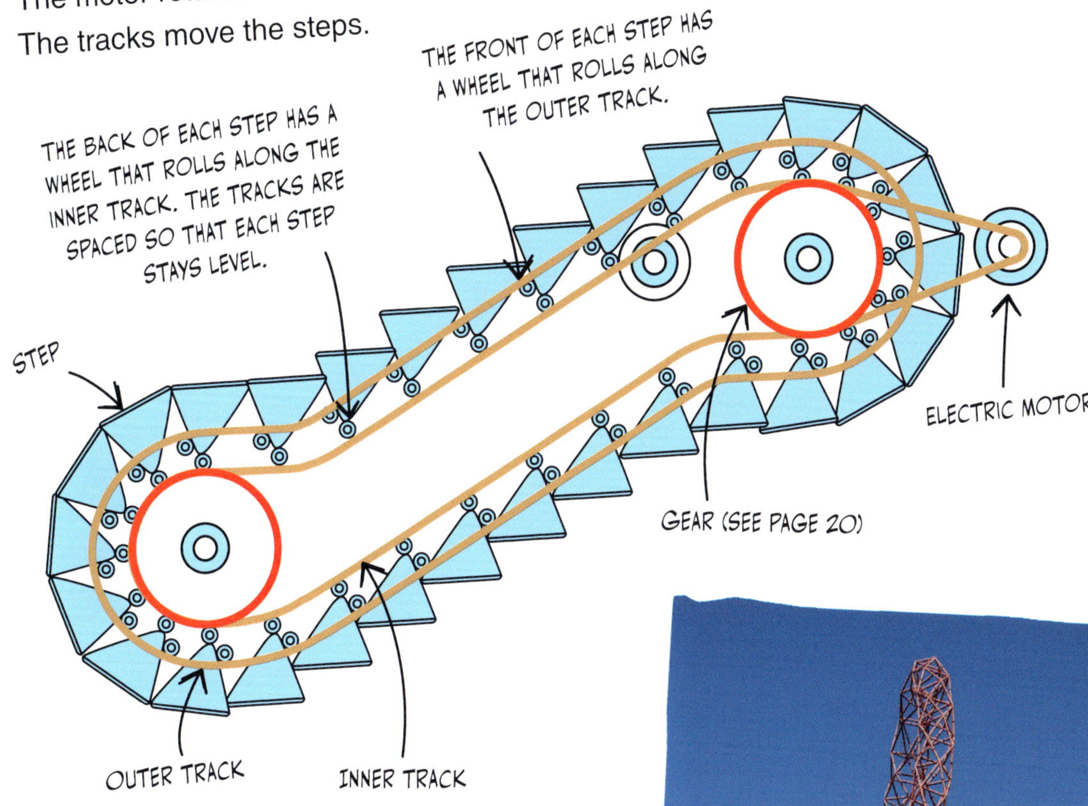

FREAKY FACT

As well as carrying people and loads upward, inclined planes can help us to descend quickly, safely – and excitingly! The world's longest tunnel slide (a twisting, enclosed inclined plane) is at the ArcelorMittal Orbit tower in London, UK. It is 584 feet (178 m) long!

AAAAARGH!

WHEELY GOOD

Without wheels, cars wouldn't get very far! The wheel, attached to a rod called an axle, is one of humanity's greatest inventions ...

WHAT'S SO CLEVER ABOUT A WHEEL AND AXLE?

The wheel and axle gives a great mechanical advantage. It is much easier to pull a load on a wheeled cart than it is to slide that load along the ground. This is partly because of all the friction between a sliding load and the ground. Friction is a force that works in the opposite direction from the way the load is traveling. There is much less friction between the narrow edge of a wheel and the ground. A wheel is also much bigger than the axle it turns around. This means that for every turn of the axle, the rim of the wheel travels a greater distance. When a cart is pulled along, the bigger the wheels, the farther and faster the cart travels – with no extra effort by the puller!

THE RIM OF A WHEEL TURNS FARTHER THAN ITS AXLE.

ARE WHEELS JUST FOR CARS AND BIKES?

Wheels are ideal for vehicles that roll along roads, paths, or tracks, such as cars, bikes, scooters, and trains. But if you look around, there are lots of other wheels in compound machines.

SUPER STEERING

WHEN A BOAT'S STEERING WHEEL IS TURNED, THE MOVEMENT IS TRANSMITTED TO THE RUDDER, A FLAP OF WOOD OR METAL THAT CHANGES ANGLE TO DEFLECT WATER, TURNING THE BOAT LEFT OR RIGHT.

TERRIFIC TURBINES

THE OCEAN'S MOVEMENT TURNS TURBINES, WHICH ARE CONNECTED TO GENERATORS. THESE CHANGE MOVEMENT ENERGY INTO ELECTRICITY, IN THE OPPOSITE PROCESS TO AN ELECTRIC MOTOR (SEE PAGE 7).

WHAT'S THE LARGEST WHEEL?

The largest wheel is an observation wheel called Ain Dubai, in the United Arab Emirates. It measures 820 feet (250 m) across. A wheel this large cannot be solid, as it would be immensely heavy. Instead, 192 metal spokes link the axle with the rim, transferring the turning force. The super-strong spokes also brace the wheel, stopping it from bending out of shape.

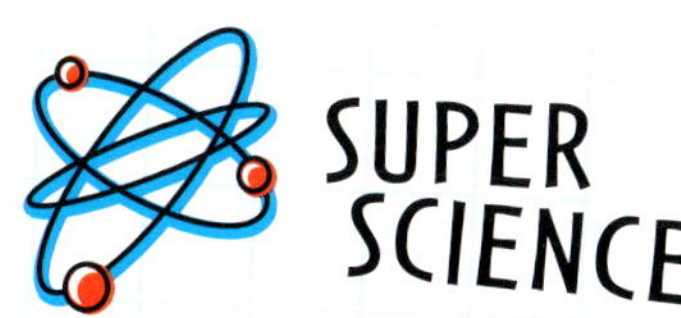

A round wheel can get stuck if a vehicle drives over rocky or uneven ground. A new invention called the Reconfigurable Wheel-Track can change wheels from circular to round-cornered triangles by pressing a button. The invention is used on military vehicles that need to veer off-road. As the triangular wheels turn, they can lift the vehicle up and over small obstacles.

SPINNING YARN

COTTON THREAD IS SPUN (STRETCHED, TWISTED, AND WOUND ONTO A BOBBIN) FROM FLUFFY COTTON SEED HEADS BY TURNING WHEELS.

CLEAN WASH

IN A WASHING MACHINE, AN ELECTRIC MOTOR TURNS A CIRCULAR DRUM, WHICH CIRCULATES SOAPY WATER THROUGH THE LAUNDRY.

(NOT SO) BORING TUNNELS

A TUNNEL BORING MACHINE HAS A HUGE, SPINNING CIRCULAR HEAD THAT IS ARMED WITH BLADES THAT SLICE THROUGH THE EARTH.

LOVELY LEVERS

A lever is a straight, unbending rod or beam, but what makes it useful is that the beam can turn (or pivot) on a point along itself. That point is called the fulcrum.

I'M LOVING THIS CLASS 1 LEVER, JIM.

WHY IS A SEESAW A MARVELOUS MACHINE?

A seesaw is a lever with a fulcrum at its center. You would find it very hard to lift a friend off the ground, but if they are sitting at the end of a seesaw, you can lift them with little effort. By sitting at the opposite end, your weight pulls your end of the lever downward. If the fulcrum of a lever is farther toward one end, a lever can give an even bigger mechanical advantage in lifting a load.

CLASS 1 LEVER

IN A CLASS 1 LEVER, THE FULCRUM IS BETWEEN THE EFFORT AND THE LOAD.

IT TAKES LESS EFFORT TO LIFT A LOAD IF THE FULCRUM IS CLOSER TO THE LOAD. THE LONG END OF THE LEVER HAS TO COVER A GREATER DISTANCE, BUT IT RESULTS IN A GREATER LIFTING FORCE ON THE LOAD.

CLASS 2 LEVER

IN A CLASS 2 LEVER, THE LOAD IS BETWEEN THE EFFORT AND THE FULCRUM.

A CLASS 2 LEVER, SUCH AS A WHEELBARROW (SEE PAGE 4), ALSO MAKES IT EASIER TO LIFT A LOAD, BUT THE EFFORT MUST BE APPLIED UPWARD.

ARE LEVERS JUST FOR LIFTING?

Levers are also useful for cutting, crushing, and holding:

CLEVER CUTTING

SCISSORS ARE CLASS 1 LEVERS. WITH LITTLE EFFORT, GREAT FORCE CAN BE PUT ON THE LOAD (PAPER) SO IT IS CUT!

CRUCIAL CRUSHING

A NUTCRACKER IS A CLASS 2 LEVER. LITTLE EFFORT IS NEEDED TO CRUSH THE LOAD, WHICH IS A NUT!

HEAVENLY HOLDING

BARBECUE TONGS BELONG TO THE 3RD AND LAST CLASS OF LEVERS. THE EFFORT IS APPLIED BETWEEN THE FULCRUM AND THE LOAD, WHICH MEANS THE TONGS DO NOT INCREASE THE FORCE - AND THE FOOD IS NOT CRUSHED! HOWEVER, TONGS DO MAKE IT EASY TO GRIP HOT FOOD!

HOW DOES A CRANE LIFT LOADS HIGH?

A crane is an example of a class 3 lever, like barbecue tongs. Although class 3 levers do not increase the lifting force on a load, they do have a mechanical advantage. For a crane, the end of the long lever carries the load much farther than the distance moved by the effort, lifting the load really high.

FREAKY FACT

Mechanical excavators have arms that are built from linked levers (like human arms) so they can grasp and lift heavy loads. The biggest excavator, the Bucyrus RH400, has a bucket able to hold 1,590 cubic feet (45 cubic m) of rock.

PULL A PULLEY

A pulley is a wheel with a rope, cable, or belt looped around its rim. A pulley is a hugely useful simple machine because it changes the direction of a force. If a group of pulleys are used together, they can increase a force too!

HOW DO WE RAISE FLAGS TO RECORD-BREAKING HEIGHTS?

The world's tallest flagpole is in Jeddah, Saudi Arabia. It is 561 feet (171 m) tall. The flag isn't pulled to the top of the pole by someone on a tall ladder! Like all flagpoles, this one uses a pulley, fixed in position at the top of the pole. The key advantage of a pulley is that – because the rope is looped around it – it changes the direction of a force from downward to upward. This means that someone standing on the ground pulls downward on a rope – and raises the flag attached to the other end!

PULLEY SYSTEM

I'M GOING UP ...

ELEVATOR CAR

COUNTERWEIGHT

HOW DOES AN ELEVATOR WORK?

An elevator is usually powered by an electric motor (see page 7). It uses a system of pulleys, which means the motor needs less power to raise the car. In addition, an elevator system has a counterweight, attached to the opposite end of the cable from the elevator. The counterweight weighs about as much as the elevator when it is half full of people. The counterweight pulls downward on the cable, which – thanks to the pulley system – pulls upward on the elevator. This further reduces the motor's work when it is raising the elevator. When the elevator is descending, the counterweight stops it from racing out of control due to the downward force of gravity.

HOW DO PULLEYS HELP US LIFT HEAVIER LOADS?

If a load is attached to the end of a rope, a pulley system can increase the user's pulling force:

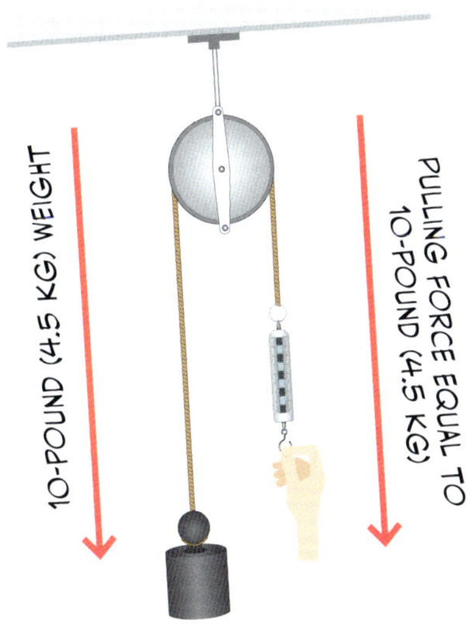

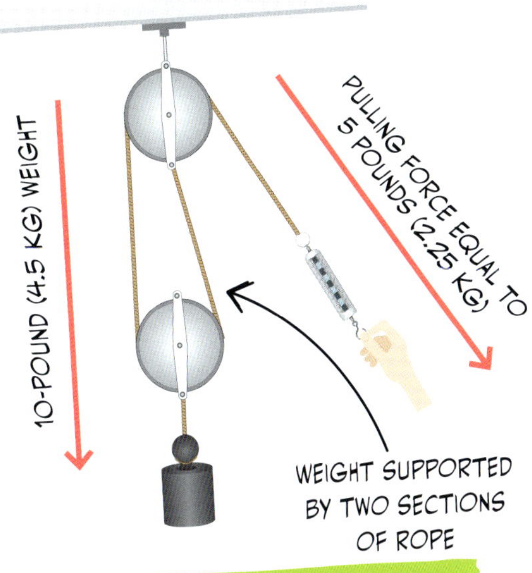

USEFUL

A SINGLE PULLEY DOES NOT INCREASE THE USER'S PULLING FORCE. YOU WILL NEED TO PULL THE ROPE 3 FEET (0.9 M) TO LIFT THE LOAD BY 3 FEET (0.9 M).

MORE USEFUL

BY ADDING A SECOND PULLEY, THE 10-POUND (4.5 KG) WEIGHT IS SUPPORTED BY TWO SECTIONS OF ROPE. IT NOW TAKES ONLY 5 POUNDS (2.25 KG) WORTH OF EFFORT TO LIFT THE LOAD. HOWEVER, TO LIFT THE LOAD BY 3 FEET (0.9 M), YOU WILL NEED TO PULL THE ROPE 6 FEET (1.8 M).

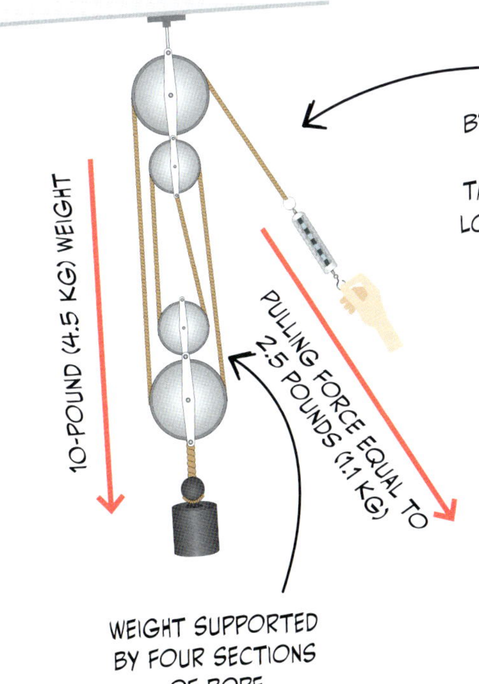

EVEN MORE USEFUL

BY USING FOUR PULLEYS, THE 10-POUND (4.5 KG) WEIGHT IS SUPPORTED BY FOUR SECTIONS OF ROPE. IT NOW TAKES ONLY 2.5 POUNDS (1.1 KG) OF EFFORT TO LIFT THE LOAD. HOWEVER, TO LIFT THE LOAD BY 3 FEET (0.9 M), YOU WILL NEED TO PULL THE ROPE 12 FEET (3.7 M).

FREAKY FACT

The world's tallest elevator is in the Mponeng Gold Mine in South Africa. It carries miners 7,490 feet (2,283 m) beneath Earth's surface at speeds of up to 40 mph (64 kph).

SCREW IT IN

A screw is a shaft with a spiraling groove (called threads) around its outside. This simple machine changes a turning motion into forward motion. The screw was the last simple machine to be invented ... at least 2,600 years ago!

WHY DO CARPENTERS USE SCREWS?

A carpenter uses screws to hold pieces of wood together. A screw is actually a pole with an inclined plane (see page 10) wrapped around it. Like all simple machines, a screw offers a mechanical advantage. It takes less strength to screw in a screw (by turning it with a screwdriver) than it does to bang in a nail to the same depth. This is because a screw spreads the user's effort over a longer distance (all the way along the spiraling groove). Each complete turn of the screw head produces a movement of only one thread of the screw tip into the wood. The carpenter's work takes longer, but is less difficult!

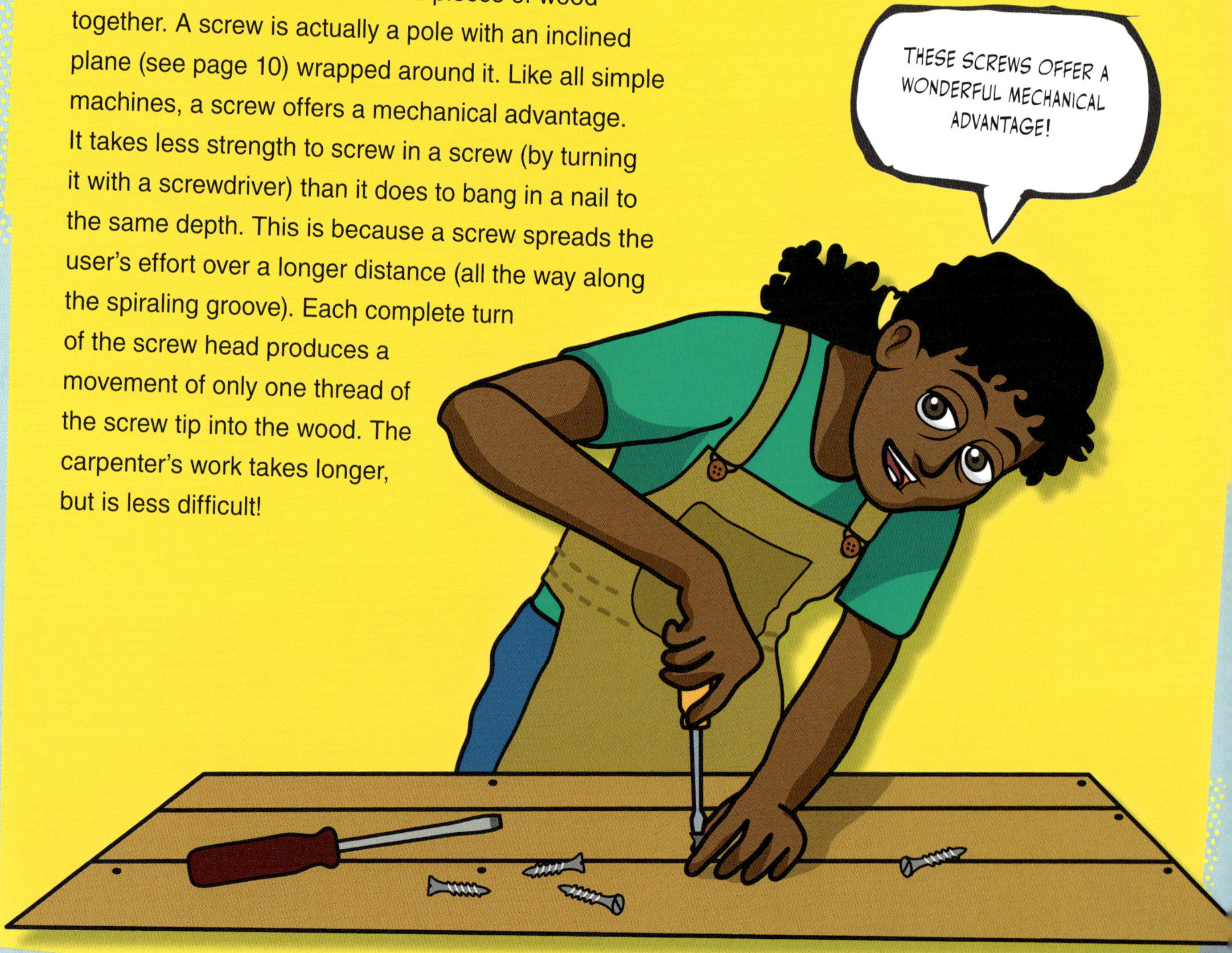

WHAT DIDN'T ARCHIMEDES INVENT?

The inventor Archimedes (c.287–212 BCE) did not invent the Archimedes' screw! However, he did write about the marvelous machine that is named after him, when he saw one at work in Egypt. The screw was lifting water from the River Nile into a ditch, from where it flowed to the fields to water crops. In this machine, the screw is inside a tube, which is placed in water. As the screw is turned, its threads lift water up the tube.

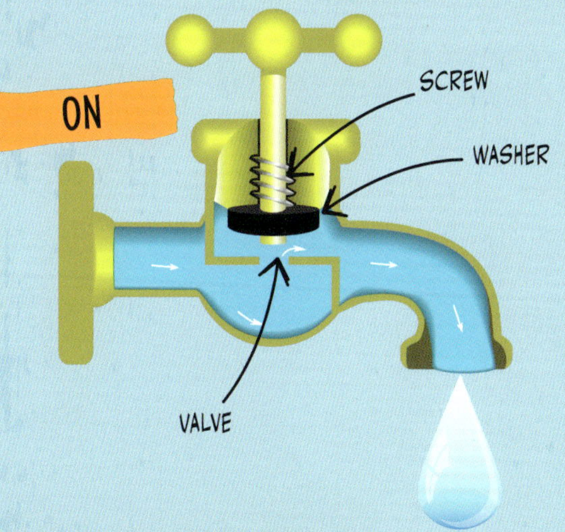

THE SCREW-DOWN TAP MECHANISM WAS INVENTED IN 1845 BY BRITISH BRASS TAP MAKERS GUEST AND CHRIMES.

HOW DO SCREWS HELP US TO WASH OUR HANDS?

When you turn on a tap to wash your hands, you are turning a screw. Just as it is hard to bang a nail into a wall, it would be hard to stop the flow of water from a tap without using a screw mechanism. The turning of the screw presses a flat ring, called a washer, against a valve – or moves it away again.

FREAKY FACT

An Archimedes' screw-type mechanism can be used to carry more than water. Screw conveyors are used to move solid human waste in water treatment plants, where sewage water is treated and cleaned.

GO UP A GEAR

You will find gears in many machines, from vehicles to electric motors. Gears are wheels with teeth cut into their edges. Gears are great because they can be fit together to change the speed, force, or direction of a power source.

WHAT'S GOOD ABOUT GEARS?

When gears of different sizes are fit together, they can do amazing things. Gears do not make energy – they just transfer it in a useful way ...

FASTER!

THE BIG GEAR HAS 20 TEETH, BUT THE LITTLE GEAR HAS 10 TEETH. ONE TURN OF THE BIG GEAR MAKES THE LITTLE GEAR TURN TWICE. THE LITTLE GEAR TURNS TWICE AS FAST TO KEEP UP! THIS TYPE OF GEAR ARRANGEMENT IS USEFUL FOR INCREASING THE SPEED OF A MOVEMENT.

MORE FORCE!

ONE TURN OF THE LITTLE WHEEL MAKES THE BIG WHEEL GIVE A HALF-TURN. THE BIG WHEEL TURNS SLOWER BUT WITH MORE FORCE. THIS TYPE OF GEAR ARRANGEMENT IS USEFUL WHEN DRIVING A TRUCK UP A HILL – THE TRUCK NEEDS FORCE RATHER THAN SPEED.

HOW DOES A CAN OPENER WORK?

A CAN OPENER COMBINES GEARS, A LEVER (THE HANDLES), AND A WEDGE (THE EDGE OF THE CUTTING WHEEL).

A wheeled can opener makes use of several simple machines. The first machine is a lever: the handles. To open a can, you must first separate the handles. As you close the lever, little effort is needed to press the cutting wheel through the lid of the can. The second simple machine is a wedge: the sharp edge of the cutting wheel. The third simple machine is a set of gears. When you turn the opener's key, it turns a gear called the traction gear. This gear's teeth connect with the teeth of the cutting wheel. As the traction gear rotates the can, the cutting wheel cuts open the lid.

WHEN ARE WORMS USEFUL?

A worm gear is a gear shaped like a screw. Its threads connect with the teeth of a circular gear. Worm gears are useful for changing the direction of a turning movement.

IN THIS FACTORY MACHINE, A CIRCULAR MOVEMENT IS TURNED INTO THE LINEAR (STRAIGHT) MOVEMENT OF A RACK BY A WORM GEAR.

A GUITAR'S STRINGS ARE TUNED BY TURNING KEYS, WHICH TURN WORM GEARS, WHICH TURN CIRCULAR GEARS THAT TIGHTEN OR LOOSEN THE WOUND STRINGS.

American sculptor and engineer Arthur Ganson has designed an amazing series of gears. Although the first gears in the series are turning fast enough for us to see their movement, the gears interlock in such a way that the last gear in the series will take 13.7 billion years to make one full rotation. This is the estimated age of the universe, giving the viewer an insight into the difficult-to-understand vastness of both time and space.

ROUND AND ROUND

Engines produce a back-and-forth motion, while electric motors make a round and round motion (see pages 6–7). But what does an inventor do if they need an engine to turn a wheel or a motor to push a piston? They can use a crank or a cam!

WHAT IS A CRANK?

A crank is a rod that can turn a back-and-forth motion into a circular motion. It can connect a piston to a wheel. The crank connects to the edge of the wheel, so that as the piston moves forward, the crank gives the wheel a half-turn. As the piston moves back, the crank gives the wheel another half-turn in the same direction. A car engine usually has four pistons, which together turn a slightly more complicated crankshaft.

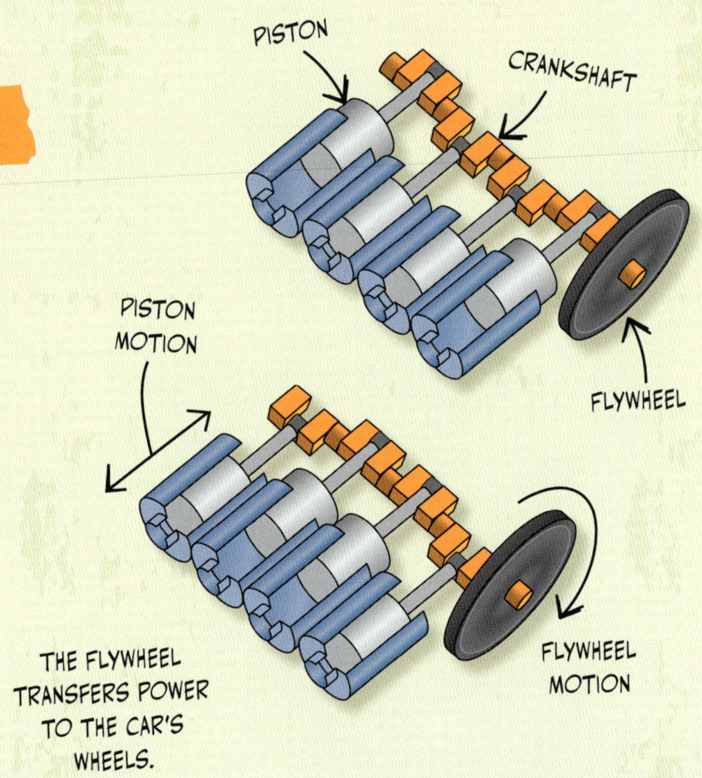

HOW DOES A KEY UNLOCK A DOOR?

A cam usually does the opposite to a crank: it changes turning motion into back-and-forth motion. In the simplest cams, the rod that needs to move back and forth rests on top of an oval wheel – the cam. As the cam rotates, the rod rises up and down. Door locks make use of cams. When a key turns in a lock, its notches connect exactly with a series of cams, which pushes the bolt out of the way and unlocks the door.

HOW DOES AN ELECTRIC TOOTHBRUSH WORK?

Like many household devices, an electric toothbrush is powered by an electric motor. In most brushes, the round-and-round (rotary) motion of the motor is turned into a back-and-forth (oscillating) motion by a crank. The motor turns very fast, too fast for your teeth and gums, so its motion is also slowed down by gears: a small gear connects with a bigger gear, which turns more slowly (see page 20).

ROTARY MOTION CAN BE TURNED INTO OSCILLATING MOTION BY PIVOTING RODS.

SUPER SCIENCE

Today, cams and cranks are found in the joints of prosthetic limbs, used by people who do not have an arm or leg. These mechanisms allow their users to have different types of motion in different joints, with rotary motion in their wrist and lever-like motion in their elbow. Many modern prosthetic limbs can be controlled by devices that change the user's muscle movements (such as the movement of a shoulder muscle) to electrical signals.

SPRINGY SPRINGS

Springs are wobbling, bending, and squeezing in all sorts of machines, from pens to cars. A spring is a coiled wire, usually made from metal. The useful thing about a spring is that it can be stretched or squeezed ...

WHAT CAN A SPRING DO?

A spring is elastic, which means it is able to return to its original shape if it is stretched or compressed (squeezed). A spring's elasticity means that it can store and release energy. When you compress or stretch a spring, you are storing energy. When you stop compressing or stretching the spring, it returns to its original length – turning that stored energy into movement. This movement can be used by a machine to do work.

A POP-UP TOY CONTAINS A SPRING. COMPRESS THE SPRING, THEN WATCH THE TOY JUMP!

WHERE ARE SPRINGS HIDING?

TOASTERS

WHEN A TOASTER'S TIMER HAS FINISHED, IT RELEASES COMPRESSED SPRINGS, WHICH SEND A TRAY SHOOTING UPWARD - WITH YOUR TOAST!

CARS

THE SPRINGS IN A CAR'S SUSPENSION ABSORB SOME MOVEMENT ENERGY, STOPPING PASSENGERS FROM BOUNCING AROUND TOO MUCH OVER BUMPS. THE SPRINGS USE UP SOME OF THE MOVEMENT ENERGY AS THEY ARE BENT AND TWISTED.

WHICH SPRING KEEPS YOU SAFE IN THE DARK?

Clockwork machines are often powered by the energy stored in springs. A clockwork flashlight is perfect for helping people to see in places where there is not a reliable supply of electricity. To switch on the flashlight, the user turns a handle. This turning movement stores energy in a spring by winding it around a spool, called the storage spool. As the spring unwinds, it winds onto another spool, called the torque spool. The turning of this spool rotates a metal wire inside a magnetic field, which generates an electric current in the wire. This powers the light's bulb.

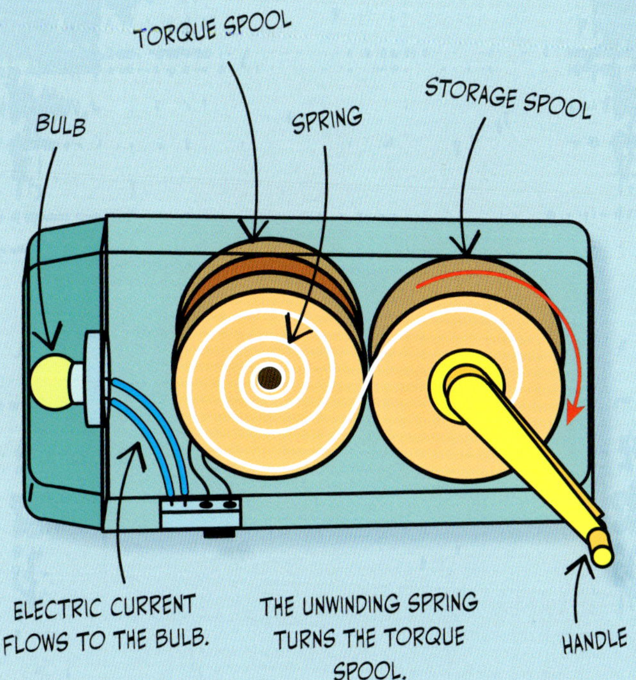

FREAKY FACT

Springs just .0036 inch (.092 mm) thick, about the same width as a hair, have been built for use in medical devices. They are found in endoscopes, which are long, thin tubes with a camera at one end that are used to look deep inside the body.

TRAMPOLINES

A TRAMPOLINE'S ELASTICITY IS GIVEN BY THE MANY SPRINGS THAT CONNECT THE FABRIC TO THE RIGID FRAME. WHEN YOUR JUMP EXERTS FORCE ON THE SPRINGS, THEY EXTEND. BUT THE SPRINGS THEN PUSH BACK WITH THE SAME FORCE YOU EXERTED – SENDING YOU BOUNCING UPWARD!

BALLPOINT PENS

IN A RETRACTABLE PEN, WHICH CAN BE CLICKED ON AND OFF WITH A BUTTON, A SPRING PUSHES THE PEN TIP INTO A WRITING POSITION WHEN THE BUTTON IS PRESSED.

FABULOUS FLUIDS

Some amazing machines are moved by fluids. A fluid is a gas or liquid. The advantage of fluids is that they can flow! Machines moved by flowing gases are called pneumatic, while those moved by flowing liquid are called hydraulic.

HOW DOES FLUID MOVE MACHINES?

Most pneumatic and hydraulic machines are powered by an electric motor or an engine. A pneumatic machine uses air or a gas such as nitrogen. The gas is pushed through the machine by a compressor, which is powered by the motor or engine. A hydraulic machine uses a liquid, such as water or oil. The fluid is pushed through the machine by a pump. The pressure of the gas or liquid pushes against valves and pistons, making the machine move.

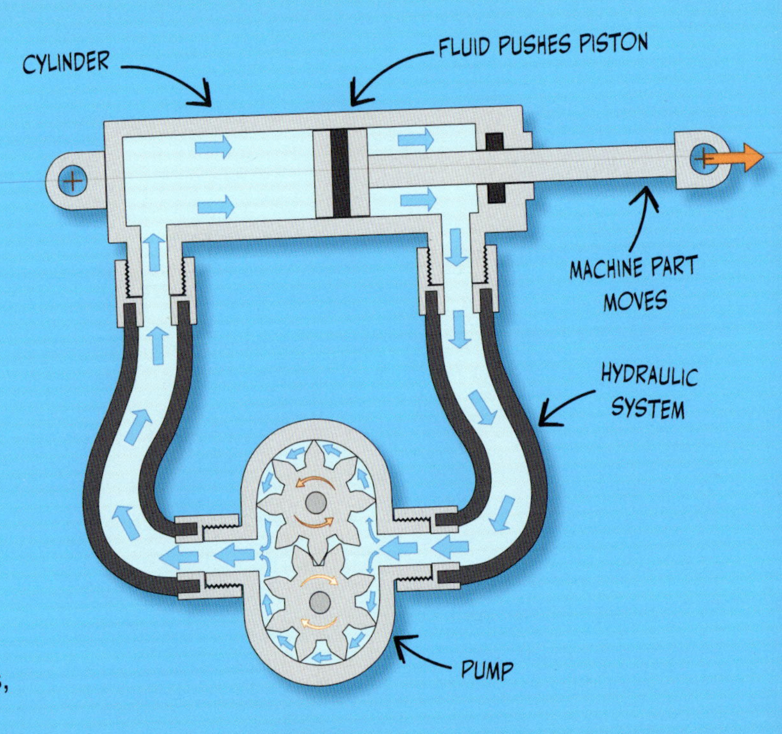

HOW DO PNEUMATIC TUBES HELP HOSPITALS?

AND OFF WE GO ... WHEEEEEEEE!

A pneumatic tube is a hollow shaft through which containers are pushed by compressed air. These tube systems are often used in hospitals to carry samples, such as blood, from one department to another. This is much quicker and easier than a person carrying samples up and down stairs. Containers can travel at 25 ft (7.5 m) per second, but pneumatic systems can also be very gentle, with changes in air pressure used for braking so that containers are not broken.

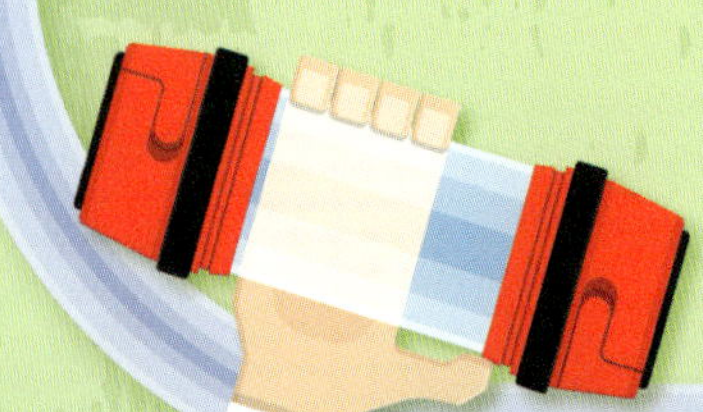

WHY ARE RESCUE TOOLS POWERED BY LIQUID?

Hydraulic machines can be very powerful, able to lift heavy loads or drill through concrete. A hydraulic system also has fewer moving parts than a machine in which force is transmitted by cranks, springs, and gears. This means a hydraulic machine can be long-lasting and reliable. If a hydraulic machine uses water or another liquid that does not burn, it is safe to use in mines, in chemical plants, and at the scene of accidents. For all these reasons, hydraulics are often used for rescue tools, as well as construction machinery and vehicle braking systems.

FIRE AND AMBULANCE WORKERS CARRY OUT A PRACTICE RESCUE USING A HYDRAULIC CUTTING TOOL.

FREAKY FACT

Some modern roller coasters use pneumatic launch systems. A burst of compressed air is used to blast the roller coaster along the track. Japan's Do-Dodonpa accelerates from 0 to 112 mph (180 kph) in 1.56 seconds, the fastest launch of any roller coaster in the world.

ASTONISHING ACTIVITY: BUILD A CATAPULT

A catapult is a machine that uses a lever to fire objects! The earliest catapults, built in China around the 4th century BCE, were weapons. We will make a catapult that fires marshmallows to find out more about levers and mechanical advantage.

YOU WILL NEED:

10 WOODEN CRAFT STICKS

4 STRONG ELASTIC BANDS

A LARGE BOTTLE CAP

DOUBLE-SIDED STICKY TAPE

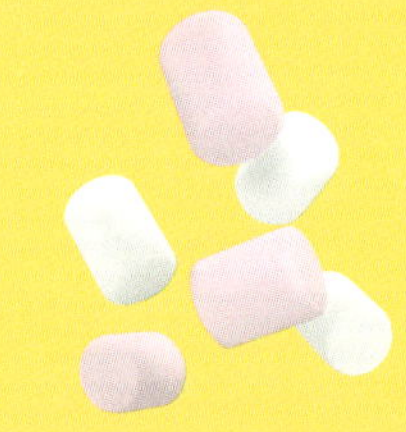

A BAG OF MARSHMALLOWS

MEASURING TAPE

PENCIL AND PAPER

WARNING: DON'T EAT MARSHMALLOWS THAT HAVE LANDED ON THE FLOOR OR BEEN HANDLED!

1. Lay five of your craft sticks on top of each other. Twist an elastic band around each end so the sticks are held tightly together.

2. Place one craft stick below the pile and one on top of the pile, at right angles – so that the sticks form a cross. These two craft sticks are going to be your lever arm. Twist an elastic band around the center of the cross so the craft sticks are joined.

REMEMBER: DO NOT SWAP THE SOFT MARSHMALLOWS FOR ANY OBJECT THAT COULD INJURE SOMEONE!

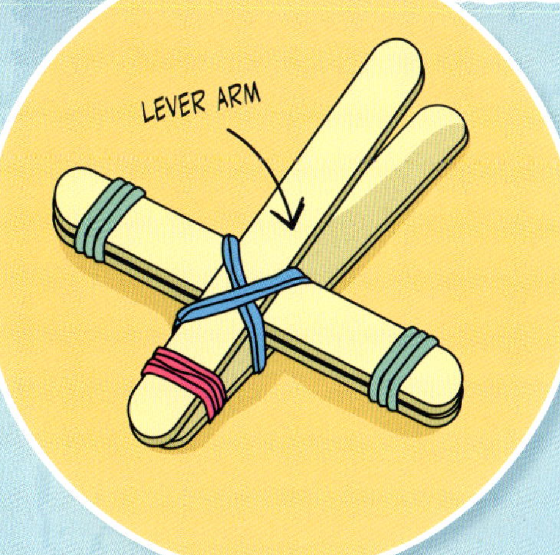

3. Twist an elastic band (shown here in pink) around one end of the lever arm.

4. Using double-sided tape, stick a large bottle cap at the other end of the lever arm from the elastic band.

5. Now let's do a test launch. Put a marshmallow in the bottle cap. While pressing down a little on the front of your catapult to hold it steady, press the bottle cap down – then release it. The marshmallow should fly through the air!

6. Now lay out your measuring tape so you can measure how far your catapult flings the next marshmallow. Write down the distance the marshmallow flies.

7. Let's adjust the machine to give the greatest mechanical advantage. What happens if you move the lever arm so there is a greater or lesser distance between the center of the cross and the bottle top? What happens if you add more or fewer craft sticks to the stack of five sticks? Write down how far your marshmallow flies with each arrangement. What works best?

RAVISHING RESULTS

When you pressed your bottle cap down, you stored energy in the bent craft stick, just like many machines store energy in springs (see page 24). When you stopped pressing, the craft stick sprang back to its original position, sending the marshmallow flying. As we learned, a lever reduces the amount of force needed to lift (or fling) a load (see page 14). The fulcrum of our lever was at the center of the cross. The greater the distance between the fulcrum and the marshmallow load, the greater the mechanical advantage and the farther the marshmallow flew. Adding more sticks to the center of the catapult made it harder to bend the end of the lever all the way down, stored more energy in the craft stick – and also sent the marshmallow farther!

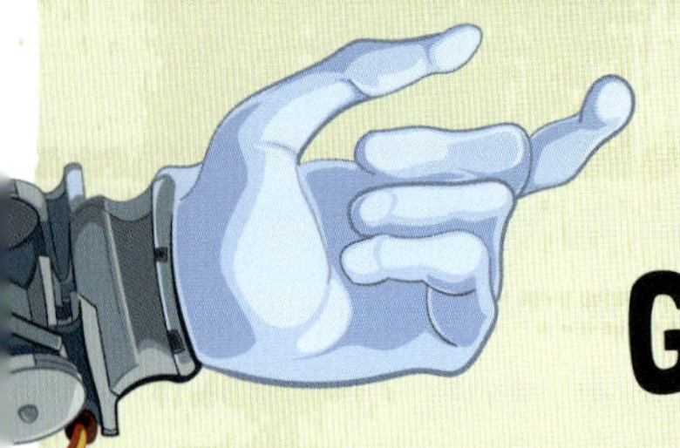

GLOSSARY

atom the smallest part of any substance that can exist on its own

axle a rod passing through the center of a wheel or group of wheels

compound machine a machine that consists of more than one simple machine

compress to squeeze

deflect to make something change direction

electricity energy resulting from charged electons and protons, which are tiny particles found in atoms

electric motor a machine that turns electricity into movement

energy the power to do work

engine a machine that changes one or more forms of energy, such as fuel, into movement

fluid a liquid, gas, or other substance that has no fixed shape

force a push or pull; a force makes an object change its motion

friction a force that resists the movement of two surfaces trying to slide across each other

fuel a material that can be burned to produce heat

gas a substance with no fixed shape or volume that will expand to fill any container

gear a toothed wheel that fits together with other gears to transmit a turning force while changing its speed

gravity a force that pulls all objects toward each other; the larger the object, the greater the pull of its gravity

hydraulic describes a system that makes use of liquid, such as water, in a confined space and under pressure

inclined plane a flat surface that is tilted at an angle

input force the force used to get a machine to begin working

lever a bar that can pivot (or turn) at a fixed hinge, called a fulcrum

liquid a substance that flows freely but has a constant volume

machine an object or group of connected objects that can pass on or change a force in order to carry out work

mechanical advantage a measure of the increase in force offered by a machine

molecular relating to molecules, which are groups of linked atoms

output force the force exerted (or put out) by a machine

piston a machine part that moves up and down, usually inside a cylinder or tube

pneumatic describes a system that makes use of gas, such as air, in a confined space and under pressure

power to supply with energy

power station a place where electricity is made, by burning fuels such as coal or by using nuclear, wind, water, or solar power

pressure a pushing force

pulley a wheel with a grooved rim around which a cord passes

screw a cyclinder with a raised spiraling thread running around it

simple machine a basic device that changes the direction or strength of a force. The simple machines are the wheel, wedge, inclined plane, screw, lever, and pulley

turbine a wheel-like device that is turned by liquid or gas

valve a device that opens and closes to control the flow of fluid

wedge an object with a pointed edge at one end and a wide edge at the other

work using a force to move an object, or transferring energy from one object to another

FURTHER READING

BOOKS

Forces in Action: Balance, Motion and Levers (Science Is Everywhere),
Rob Colson (Wayland, 2019)

Machines and Motors (Infographic: How it Works),
Jon Richards and Ed Simkins (Wayland, 2016)

Working with Machines (Kid Engineer),
Sonya Newland (Wayland, 2021)

WEBSITES

Find out more about machines on these websites:
https://sciencestruck.com/simple-machines-for-kids

www.britannica.com/technology/steam-engine

www.ducksters.com/science/physics/work.php

INDEX